Nimrod

"The Mighty Hunter Before God"
Genesis 10:8-12; Micah 5:6

How Religions Began

Charts Included

H.A.Lewis

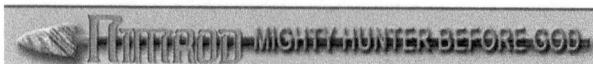

Nimrod - How Religions Began

ISBN: 978-0-9904360-1-0   Soft cover

This *simple* book will cause you to look into what is happening in the world today which includes the middle east,the rise of *false religions, racial wars, ecenumical order* and the *coming of the anti-christ*

Once again, **ONE** man changed the course of the world. This **ONE** man became the founder of **every false religion** we have in the world today. In fact, you can trace the history of all cults and occult back to this man. He led men into rebellion, and once again mankind was turning his back on God.

From him and his wife comes the legend of the Egyptian god and goddess **Osiris** and his consort **Isis** .(pg 27)

Modern terrorist groups take the name of Isis, the Egyptian goddess and it is also **the name of Jesus** as written in the Koran

The flooding of the entire Earth, was a chance for re-birthing the planet and an opportunity for righteousness to permeate the Earth again, **but** Nimrod instituted rebellion and witchcraft, placing himself at the ancestral root of the anti-Christ.

Contents

Part 1

Chapter 1................................7

Chapter 2................................11

Chapter 3................................15

Chapter 4................................23

Part II

Chapter 5..............................27

Chapter 6..............................33

Chapter 7..............................37

Chapter 8..............................45

One life, one decision, one action can change the course of a government, the ways of a nation, or the religion of the entire world... that ONE was Nimrod.

Chapter 1

One action, one decision, one life can completely
change the course of a government, an entire nation
or the world. The change will always be immense
whether it is an honorable or destructive one. To
understand the magnitude of how the life of one man
changed the course of the entire world we must
ascertain the events of the world before this particular
man came on the scene. **Genesis 6:2** states that it
came to pass that the sons of God saw that the
daughters of men were fair to look upon; therefore,
they took to them wives, as many as they chose to.
Seeing this act of rebellion, the Lord said, "My Spirit
shall not always strive with man, for their days shall
be a hundred and twenty years." **Genesis 6:3**
Continuing on in the Scriptures we find that there
were giants in the earth in the days before and after
the flood of *Noah*. The sons of God, known also as
the fallen angels, came unto the daughters of men.
This unlawful union between the fallen angels and the
daughters of men produced giants - mutated offspring
which became mighty men of old and renown. These
mutated offspring were all over the populated earth
and were known by many names. Just as we reference
men by their many nationalities, even though they are
still of the same species (created man), so it was with
these giants.

They were known in the Hebrew language as *Nephilim - giants*, bullies or tyrants. Also, the Hebrew word *gibbor* was used to show physical size and strength, strong men **Job 16:14**. Another name for these mutated offspring was *Anakims* - a people great and tall (**Deuteronomy 1:28; 2:10-11, 21; 9:2; Joshua 11:21-22; 14:12-14**). The land of Ammon was the land of the giants for they dwelt there in the days of old.

Besides being known as *Anakims*, they were also called *Emins*. In fact, the *Emins* were as great and as tall as the *Anakims* **Deuteronomy 2:10-11**. Later on in **Deuteronomy 2:19-21**, we find them known as the *Zanzummins*. In **Deuteronomy 3**, we are introduced to *Og* - the king of the giants in *Bashan*. It is said that his bed was about eighteen and a half feet long and eight feet and four inches wide.

Indeed these *mutated half-breeds* of the sons of God and the daughters of men were truly unusual. Along with the names previously mentioned, they were also known as *rephaims*. Therefore, the land of the giants can be properly called the remnant of the *rephaim*. The following are other names given to these creatures: *Kenites, Kenizzite, Kadomites, Hittites, Perizzites, Canaanites, Girgashites, Jebusites* (**Genesis 6:2; 14:5-6; 15:19-21; Exodus 3:8, 17; 23:23; Deuteronomy 2:20-23; 3:11-13; 7:1; 20:17; Joshua 12:4-8; 13:14; 15:8; 15:15; 18:16**)

The corruption of the human race grieved God. He saw that every intention of man's heart was evil and the wickedness of man was great upon the earth. It troubled the Lord so much He repented that he made man upon the earth. His heart so mourned over such corruption that He said he would destroy man from off the face of the earth. Not only would He destroy man, but He would destroy all the beasts and the creeping things on the planet, as well as the fowl of the air.

Although God was righteously angry, He held back His hand from destroying all mankind because of one righteous man by the name of *Noah.* Praise God *Noah* found grace in the eyes of God! If he had not, more than likely we wouldn't be here today. It just took one man to affect the outcome for all of mankind. In *Noah's* case, it was his righteousness. Because of that, God spared the extinction of mankind.

Lets take a moment and try to imagine just how wicked and evil man had gotten before the flood. They were so vile and reprehensible God no longer considered them fit to continue on the earth. In fact, their wickedness was getting ready to affect the whole creation. God was angry. He was so angry that He concluded that every thought of man's heart and imagination was corrupt and evil. Every man was living for himself and did not care about God. The entire earth was rotten at this time except for one man - *Noah.*

Now, because of the righteousness of *Noah*, God had mercy on him and gave him the plans that would spare his family from the coming destruction.

The Bible does **not** state that *Noah's* family was righteous. It just mentions *Noah's* name. Amazing! Take this fact into consideration for today. If you live for God and are righteous, and you serve an obey Him, He will not only spare you,

 He will even save your entire family **Acts 2:38-39**. Remember, God is merciful to those who love Him.

Chapter 2

In the very beginning we covered a theological view of where the giants in the Scriptures came from. It is also important to note that these mutants would be the foundation of the gods and goddesses of mythology and of the religions of the world. The *uncanonized* book of **Enoch I** is extremely insightful when it comes to the study of these giants that were a result of the union between the sons of God and the daughters of men.

There is another theological point of view that argues against the concept of the sons of God being *fallen angels*. This particular point of view argues that the sons of God were the righteous lineages of **Seth**, the **son of Adam and Eve**. **Seth** replaced **Abel** who was killed by his brother **Cain**. The daughters of men were the daughters of the unrighteous line of Cain.

What exactly is the theological view saying? It states that the vast corruption of this world took place in **Genesis 6** by the intermarriage between the sons of **Seth**, the righteous lineage and the daughters of **Cain**, the unrighteous line. In other words, the physical relation between two normal human beings produced giant offspring. I have a problem with this point of view because it is stating that in order to give birth to a giant like **Og** or **Goliath**, a Godly man is to reproduce with an ungodly woman. The result would be mutated offspring. Somehow I find this theological view lacking.

Keep in mind also that in three hundred and twenty years of the recorded genealogy of the lineage of Seth there were only three men considered righteous - **Seth, Enoch** and **Noah**. How could they have populated the whole world? In **Genesis 4:26** at the time **Enosh**, the **son of Seth**, was born, men began to call on the name of **Jehovah**. What it says in the *Hebrew* is that man began to call himself by the name of God or to give God's name to their idols.

Finally, if the lineage of **Cain** and **Seth** was necessary in order to produce offspring that were giants, then how do we explain the giants born after the flood? After all, the *daughters* of **Cain** and the sons of **Seth** were drowned in the flood with the exception of *Noah* and his family who were of the lineage of **Seth**. There were **no** more daughters of **Cain.** They were gone. How could these new giants be the product of the mixed marriage of two human lines?

No matter what viewpoint you choose to believe, the fact is simply that the whole world was in unrighteousness and man rebelled against the God of creation. Man decided he would do whatever he wanted to do. *He didn't fear judgment at all.* The world now stunk in the nostrils of God. And God was determined not to allow this rebellion. Not only was He going to destroy mankind, but all of His creation.

Because of the obedience of this one man, *Noah*, salvation was brought to mankind.

If he had not humbled himself, or chosen not to follow God and did what was right in the eyes of God, then nothing would have survived.

You and I would not be here today. I would not be writing this book, and you would not be reading it.

We can only speculate what would have happened had **Noah** been unrighteous. Like other planets in our solar system, Earth could have become uninhabitable. Quite possibly, God would have had to start all over again in another solar system or galaxy. Only God knows what the outcome to this planet would have been.

Speculation aside, we can praise God that there was one man who was willing to humble himself in the presence of an almighty God. Because of **Noah** we were spared and now have this wonderful opportunity to serve God and to be made righteous.

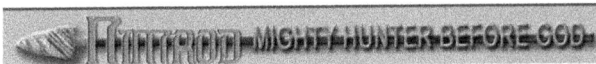

Though God found **ONE** righteous man, He did judge
the earth.

God cannot allow disrespect, sin or rebellion. He
must pass judgment because He is a holy, righteous
and pure God. Evil is not allowed in His presence. It
must be dealt with. It is His law. If you break the law,
you have to pay for breaking it.

*God knew He had to come Himself to pay the price to
redeem man from the curse. He sent His Son, Jesus,
to pay that price. No other god would be willing to
send his own son to take our place, but the one true
God did. What a God of love! For without the
shedding of blood there is no remission or
forgiveness of sin **Hebrews 9:2**. There had to be
restored fellowship with God.*

***Please Note:** Because of **ONE man who was willing
to obey** the Father in all things,it became possible for
mankind to come back to God.*

For with God nothing shall be impossible **Luke 1:37**

We had become separated from God because of the actions of one man, **Adam**. He disobeyed and rebelled against God - bringing the entire world into chaos, judgment and under subjection to sin. Noah was this one man who saved mankind, but it was only physically. Jesus, however, made it possible for mankind to be saved - spirit, soul and body. It was complete salvation, and because of that we can be safe from the judgment which is to come in the near future.

Chapter 3

In **Genesis 10** God begins to speak about another man. His name was **Cush**. He was the son of **Ham** and the *grandson* of **Noah**. He had a son named *Nimrod*. **Genesis 10:8** states that *Nimrod* began to be a mighty hunter before God. Do you recall the condition of the earth before *Nimrod* came to power?

The whole earth was exceedingly wicked and God became angry. He found **Noah** to be the only righteous one, so He told him to build an ark. It took **Noah** a considerable length of time to accomplish such a huge task. When it was finally completed, God brought **Noah** and his family into the ark along with the animals - two by two (those animals that would not be eaten or used for sacrifice) and by seven (those animals that would be used for food and sacrifice). Once they were all safely inside, God personally closed the door to the ark. For the first time in the history of the whole earth, it rained; before the flood there had been no rain. A mist that rose up constantly from the ground had watered the earth - kind of like dew you see every morning.

Now for the first time, the heavens were opened and a torrent of rain began to fall. Not only did the heavens open up, but also the deep of the earth was allowed to open.

The picture here is that water came upward from the deep as well as downward from the heavens. This happened for forty days and nights until the earth was completely covered by water.

Total destruction came to every living creature on the earth except for the eight human beings and the animals that were on the ark. God preserved them so that His Creation would continue to inhabit the planet.

Soon the waters began to subside and **Noah** sent out a raven which eventually did not return to the ark. Then he sent out a dove which returned to the ark with an olive branch in its mouth. This lovely bit of the olive tree let **Noah** know that the earth was once more ready to be inhabited. Eventually, God opened the door to the ark, and **Noah** and his family came out followed by the animals.

Interestingly enough, there is an old saying (a Philippine proverb in relation to the flood):

At one time the heavens were so close to the earth that man could not stand up straight. Just like the animals man had to crawl on all fours. Eventually a young hero came and began to push the heavens.

He pushed and brought the heavens to the height of a small plant. Becoming tired because of his great effort, he rested for a season. Once rested he again began to push the heavens until he had brought it to the height of a tree. Tired because of the great exertion it took to push the heavens to this height he rested again. With strength regained, he pushed the heavens to the height of a mountain. Finally after a short respite he pushed against the heavens once again with his great strength and the heavens were brought to where they are today. Man could once again stand upright on two legs.

This Philippine Proverb

shows us that at one time the presence of God was so strong on the face of the earth that man could not walk in disobedience to God and His laws. For a while man feared the judgment; after all, there had just been a cataclysmic flood. Because of the fear of judgment, mankind did not walk in arrogance, but in righteousness. The moments after the flood the whole earth had a healthy respect for God's holiness and were willingly serving Him.

Once again, **ONE man** changed the course of the world. This one man became the founder of every false religion we have in the world today.

In fact, you can trace the history of all cults and occult back to this man. He led men into rebellion, and once again mankind was turning his back on God. They no longer feared the judgment of the Lord and only did what they wanted to do. Nimrod, the son of **Cush,** *grandson* of **Ham**, and great-grandson of **Noah**, was that man.

What happened after the flood to the time *Nimrod* came on the scene with his rebellion? You see, right after the flood man was terrified. They had just been through a harrowing experience. Noah, his wife, his sons and their wives knew God kept His word. If God says He is going to bless someone, He blesses him. If God says He is going to impart judgment, judgment is passed.

Noah and his family saw that judgment. They saw God's power as they were tossed back and forth in the ark which floated on the waters covering the entire earth. They felt the strength of the storm through the walls of the ark. They remembered the screams of those that were not spared - the banging on the door to let them in. They understood that God was mighty and awesome. Nothing could stand in the way of His judgment, and no power could resist it or stand against it.

I guarantee you if **Noah** and his family were anything like we are they were shaken, afraid and in complete awe of God once they departed from the ark. I know that respect had returned to their hearts and they knew firsthand the mighty power of God's righteous judgment.

As easily as He created the world, He could destroy it. God showed mercy on His creation and sent a rainbow as a promise that a flood would not destroy the entire earth again. He wants our willing obedience, and any rebellion against His word will place Him back into the position of judge. Though it may not be a flood again, judgment will come to the entire earth if the people rebel.

Therefore **Noah** and his family were very respectful and very careful not to go against God. I do not believe **Noah** shook his fist in the face of God immediately after the flood. Neither do I believe his sons decided immediately that they were going to do things their own way. It took a season *(just as in the Philippine proverb)*.

One man's faithfulness spared the world, and one man, *Nimrod*, led the people back into rebellion. *Nimrod* became the original *anti-God* leader in the world at that time. We cannot say *anti-Christ* because Christ was not as yet incarnated in the flesh. *Nimrod* was putting himself in the place of God.

He was proclaiming himself to be divinity through his words, actions and deeds. At the time *Nimrod* was born, man did not have much security. There were no walled cities or cities like we have today.

Wild beasts were multiplying faster than man, and man was at the mercy of nature and the wild animal's attacks. Man was not warrior-like; neither did he have weapons to defend himself.

Nimrod, however, was beginning to become a mighty hunter. In other words, *Nimrod* began to slay animals, and man looked to him as a deliverer and as a strong leader. Legends recount that he killed a leopard with his bare hands - thus his nickname **Nimbus** (meaning 'the spotted'). In fact, he wore the skin of the leopard to show the strength of his victory.

Of course *Nimrod* wore the leopard skin to show others that he was so powerful not even the wild animals could stand against him. In turn, men began to respect him and be somewhat in awe of his abilities. *Nimrod* taught them how to stand against the elements and how to overcome the wild beasts. The men saw him as a great leader and desired to be like him.

Nimrod took advantage of this. Unlike his great-grandfather, Noah, Nimrod was definitely not righteous. He was not concerned about the flood or what had happened. After all, he had not lived then. Oh, he heard the stories from his grandfather, Ham and his great-grandfather, **Noah** but they were just stories from a couple of old men.

His father, **Cush**, didn't teach him righteousness or the ways of God. In fact, **Cush** for a time, was worshipped as a god called **Chaos**. Nimrod followed the way of his father and eventually outshone him, so he began to walk in his own way.

Nimrod is the young hero of the Philippine proverb. He is the one who pushed back the heavens - figuratively speaking. He did not cause men to fully rebel against God overnight. It took a season. It took him a long time to convince man he should quit looking to the heavens and instead look to him for leadership. Stories of the flood and the judgment of God had been handed down from generation to generation, so convincing people not to look to God for their needs, but to him, took *Nimrod* some time.

Step by step as in the proverb of the young hero, the heavens were pushed to the height of a plant, then a tree, a mountain and finally to where they are today. *Nimrod* was creating a huge gap between God and mankind. The earth was no longer covered in righteousness. Once again man was walking in open rebellion to the Lord Most High.

This open rebellion was accomplished, but over a period of time. It started small and seemingly insignificant but grew to an atrocious wickedness. *Nimrod* had brought man back to the conditions the earth was in before the flood. Man was doing what was right in his own sight. The people made and continued to worship to their own gods which were created in their own images. The God whose image man was created in was soon forgotten. The God of creation was no longer remembered by his own creation! And *Nimrod* was responsible! He did what the *anti-christ* will be guilty of doing - directing worship to him and taking the glory from God.

Government Structure of the Occult

BABYLONIAN BROTHERHOOD
Oldest Secret Society in Existence

Himrod
believed to
be founder

COUNCIL ON FOREIGN RELATIONS
1921

Trilateral
Commission
1972

UNA-UK
1945

ROUNDTABLE
19th century

THE ROYAL
INSTITUTE OF
INTERNATIONAL AFFAIRS
1921

Bilderberg.org
1954

Free Masons
England 1717
Founded by 2
protestant ministers
for universal brotherhood

THE CLUB OF ROME
1968

© 2017 Joshua International/H. A. Lewis Ministries

Chapter 4

According to legend, **Cush** was considered to be a god. When we look at the different translations of his name in **Babylon**, **Assyria** and **Nineveh**, we find that it is translated as **Chaos** meaning 'the shatter with a club'. **Chaos**, at one time was called the great god, the **elohim** of the **elohims**. **Chaos** was a **god above all the other gods**. Not only was **Cush** bestowed with this title, but he was also reputed to being the founder of Babylon.

It is important to note that **Cush** did not actually build the cities of **Babylon** or **Nineveh**. His son, *Nimrod*, and his **wife, Semiramis**, built them. Many of our polluted doctrines that we believe today can be attributed to Babylon and the influences of **Cush**, *Nimrod* and **Semiramis**.

Cush, for a short period of time, was known as Bel or Baal, which also means god of confusion. He enjoyed this title for a season until his son Nimrod superseded him. **Cush** didn't establish any city. He just established his evil influences.

It was *Nimrod* who built the city and fortified it with a wall. Legend, which we get from history and not the Bible, gives us proof. Scripture does not go into detail about *Nimrod*, but history and legend - especially religious history - gives us more information. For instance, the legend of **Osiris, Isis, Bacchus**, and all the gods of mythology shed light on *Nimrod's* death.

As in the case of the Greek god **Heracles** or the Roman god **Hercules**, we find out how *Nimrod* died. He had a very violent death. He was cut into many pieces, which were then sent out through all the earth as a warning to what would happen to anyone who followed the ways of *Nimrod*.

According to legend, his *grandfather*, **Ham**, was instrumental in the destruction of *Nimrod*. This son of **Noah**, who survived the flood and knew the God of creation, tried to end the idolatry, but he couldn't stop it. It grew and spread until the world was affected.

Secular history and some religious history confirm that *Nimrod's* mother was **Semiramis**. Despite their relationship, *Nimrod married his own mother* and had a **son named Tammuz**. *Nimrod's* death left Semiramis unprotected. Instead of wallowing in grief and fear, she took matters into her own hands.

She proclaimed *Nimrod* as a god and that his body was lifted from the earth and placed in the heavens. The constellation **Orion** (*the hunter*) was considered his celestial body. Now he was watching over them from the heavens. Hence, she was still under his protection. **Semiramis** took it much further and proclaimed she was the queen of heaven. Affirming she was the mother of her husband she declared their son **Tammuz** to be actually *Nimrod* incarnated. This meant their son, **Tammuz,** was really the father, *Nimrod*.

What a perversion of the Christian doctrine of the Trinity! Because of her pronouncements, Semiramis was promoted as the goddess of force or of fortitude.

Daniel 11:38 speaks of the god of fortresses, but there is **no** history of this god. History does teach about the goddess of force. The **statue of Diana** of the **Ephesians** is a statue of **Semiramis**. She is standing with a *crown around her head*, a symbol of a great wall. She earned the title goddess of fortitude because she was the one who had the great wall finished around the city of **Nineveh.**

Because of her getting the wall finished, the city became fortified from attack, and the people proclaimed her as the goddess of fortitude and force or the goddess of strength. These particular titles were given to her because of what she had accomplished or caused to come to pass. The blasphemous title, queen of heaven, was given because they believed she actually ruled from heaven alongside her husband, Nimrod, and their son,

Interesting to note that before this thought or teaching came forth, the world believed in a masculine trinity. They all held to the belief of the Father, Son and Holy Spirit. In Assyria, Babylon, Nineveh, and even Egypt you would see woodcarvings of the *triune God*. All the carvings had heads, with each head representing one of the trinity.

Semiramis came to power as a goddess and took the place of the Holy Spirit. Now she became the female side of the Father.

*(ref pg.29)*The trinity became the Father, Son and the Mother. This change is portrayed in the later woodcarvings of the *triune* god.

One head now represented the person of the Father; the second image bore a circle for the head, which stood for the sun or son. The third image had the body of a dove to show the feminine side of the god. The third person of the Godhead was now a woman, and she was equal in power to the Father and the Son. She was considered worthy to be worshipped.

Early Hindustan (or the Hindu as they are known today) believed this doctrine and had a teaching on the point of view that resembles the Babylonian doctrine of the trinity. They accepted the teaching that the third person of the trinity was a female. They believed in the father, the son as represented by the sun, and the great mother. This same philosophy or theology was believed in China and Japan. It is a false teaching that has spread throughout the entire world.

Every study you undertake, no matter what religion in the world it is, no matter the name of the god or goddess, you can trace it back to the relationship between *Nimrod* and his wife **Semiramis**

Chapter 5

Part II

Every study you undertake, no matter what religion in the world it is, no matter the name of the god or goddess, you can trace it back to the relationship between **Nimrod and his wife Semiramis.** Take the Egyptian god, **Osiris**, for example. **Osiris** and his consort **Isis**, the Egyptian sun god and moon goddess, are strikingly similar to Nimrod and **Semiramis**. Could **Ra**, who is also a sun god, be like **Tammuz**, who was considered an incarnation of Nimrod? **Osiris** and **Ra** seem to be as interchangeable as *Nimrod* and **Tammuz** were. Finally, you will see many **idols of Bast** (the cathead goddess).

In the Egyptian religion/mythology we learn that when **Osiris** or **Ra** drove his chariot across the heavens, leopards pulled it. And across his shoulders he wore a leopard skin showing his strength and authority. Sound familiar?

Let's view some other similarities

Isis wore a crown on her head, which looked like a wall. This depicted her as a goddess of fortification and force. **Isis** and **Osiris** were not only husband and wife; they were also brother and sister. Their son was also believed to be the incarnation of his father. After **Osiris'** mysterious death, his body parts were cut up and sent throughout the whole world. **Isis** searched for him for four days and found all his body parts but one, the manhood.

Therefore, in the place of the missing manhood, Isis placed a tower (**obelisk**) to show the strength of his manhood. She declared **Osiris** rose from the earth and went into the heaven, and the *constellation* **Orion** was his celestial body. Remember, Semiramis declared the body of Nimrod to be **Orion**.

Also **Osiris** and **Isis'** son *(now as the sun god)* drove his chariot across the sky to honor his father. It's amazing this legend concerning **Osiris** and his son is exactly the same legend began by **Semiramis** about Nimrod and **Tammuz**. **Orion** was now the heavenly body of *Nimrod* and his **son Tammuz** drove his chariot across the heavens in honor of his father.

Tammuz was more than just the sun god, though. According to **Semiramis**, he was actually his very own father incarnate in the flesh. This mysticism associated with *Nimrod* gave **Semiramis** the protection she needed on earth. It was easy to do since *Nimrod* had established himself so powerfully by building four great cities and unifying the world.

He became much stronger and more powerful now that he was resurrected and placed in the heavens to look down upon the earth. Because they believed the fabrication of **Semiramis**, no one dared to rebel against her. She had statues of herself and her son made and placed throughout the whole civilized world. Why? Because wherever she went she would be recognized as the great goddess of force and fortification.

Everyone would now bow before her, and everyone would follow her. Otherwise, she would be just another woman and probably killed. Back then men didn't listen to women. They ruled with an iron fist. **Semiramis** was different, though - or so they thought. She had the authority of her husband who was being worshipped as a god. Her authority was firmly established when her priest proclaimed her as the queen of heaven and equal to the father. She was now considered the third person of the holy trinity.

(ref pg26) Before **Semiramis**, the trinity consisted of the father, son, and the spirit. Images were built to symbolize the **echad** - the absolute oneness of the *Triune God*. The first was a head of an older man symbolizing the Father. The head of the second would be a circle symbolizing the seed, which would be the Son. The third image was a **dove** symbolizing the Spirit. **Semiramis**, being declared *queen of heaven, altered the holy trinity.*

The **dove** image now portrays the great mother, which symbolizes the feminine side of the great god. This false image has spread throughout the civilized world. You will find the influences and image of this warped trinity in China, Japan and India.

Even though **Semiramis** and **Tammuz** have been dead for thousands of years, the statues have remained and are still worshipped today. **Semiramis** has gone the way of all flesh. She is dead and has had to stand in front of the God of all creation, not in front of her husband who was already dead and judged. She is in hell with her husband and their son, waiting for the final judgment which is the lake of fire. She had been gone for a long, long time; however, the harm caused by the false teaching of her, *Nimrod* and **Tammuz** is still very active in the world today.

Wherever you go in the world today, in whatever religion you embrace, you will find the statue of **Semiramis** and **Tammuz**. In modern times we view them in the supposed image of *Mary* and the *Christ child.* However, this is **NOT** the true image of the *Madonna (or Mary)*, the mother of Jesus. Neither is it the image of Jesus, the Son of man and of God. Instead, these are the *images of Nimrod's wife,* the *blasphemous queen of heaven and their son, the false sun god.*

They are **NOT** the images of the"religious" holy family as people today call them. They are the most *unholy family* that ever lived.

Nimrod's rebellion and his refusal to bow to the God of creation started the greatest nightmare on the earth today - witchcraft and the occult. His actions and deeds caused the floodgates of hell to open wide on the earth. The evil beings God banished with the flood were coming back. The sons of God were once again intermixing with the daughters of men.

What does Scripture say about demon possession? The New Testament states that when the unclean spirit leaves a man, he walks through dry and barren land. Seeking rest, he finds none. The unclean spirit says, "I will return from whence I came."

Finding where he came from swept clean, he goes and finds seven worse than himself, and the latter state of the man is worse than the former **Matthew 12:43-45**. This happens to the man who was set free but refuses to accept Jesus as his Lord and allows the Holy Spirit to fill him.

Even though the Scripture does not largely address the topic of territorial spirits, I believe once you have prayed and fasted, the enemy can be driven from an area –the territory you live in or the church you fellowship with. If you allow the enemy to return to the territory, then he is not coming back alone. The latter state of your church, school, home or community will be far worse than it was before.

Remember, the earth was extremely wicked and the ONLY righteous man was Noah. The immense condition of sin on the earth was deplorable and almost unbelievable. God purifies and cleanses the earth by a flood. He sets up a new habitation for man and gives him a second chance to be free from the bondage of sin in which he was captive. Man turns his back on the generosity and mercy of God. Instead of taking advantage of the gift of God, he turns the planet back over to Satan's dominant rule.

Imagine how contemptible it was before the flood. It became more atrocious afterwards, especially when *Nimrod* established himself as a god. This act opened the door to all of Satan's schemes, devices, and every evil thing. It was bad, but now it was very bad.

Modern Witchcraft

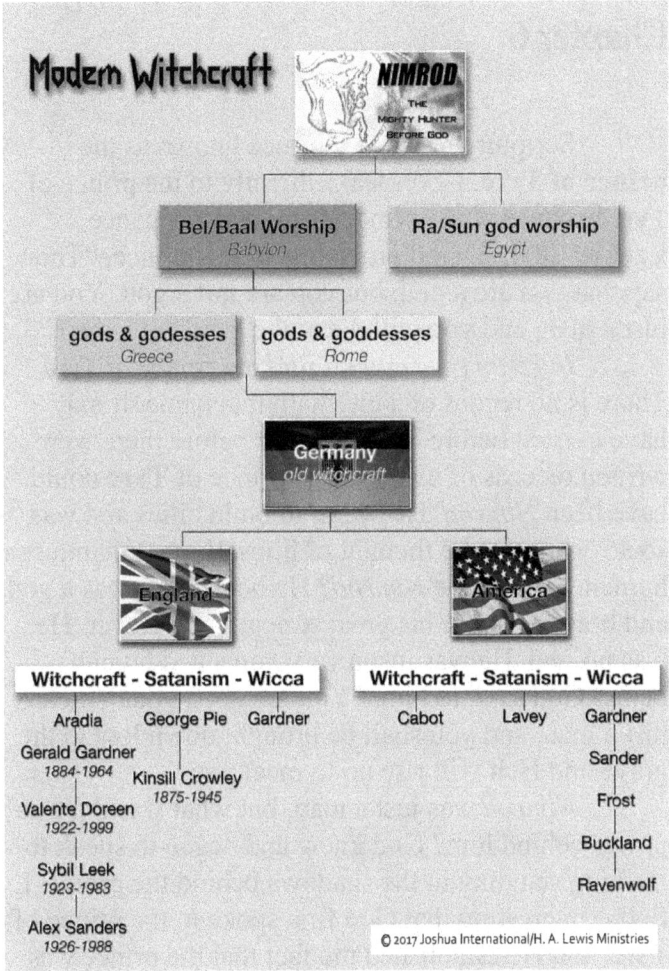

NIMROD
THE MIGHTY HUNTER BEFORE GOD

Bel/Baal Worship
Babylon

Ra/Sun god worship
Egypt

gods & godesses
Greece

gods & goddesses
Rome

Germany
old witchcraft

England

America

Witchcraft - Satanism - Wicca

Aradia   George Pie   Gardner

Gerald Gardner
1884-1964

Kinsill Crowley
1875-1945

Valente Doreen
1922-1999

Sybil Leek
1923-1983

Alex Sanders
1926-1988

Witchcraft - Satanism - Wicca

Cabot   Lavey   Gardner

Sander

Frost

Buckland

Ravenwolf

Chapter 6

Scripture refers to a prince known as the **prince of Tyre**. God speaks directly to the prince of Tyre because of the prince's ego and arrogance **Ezekiel 28:1, 2**. God proclaims to this prince, "Thou say that you are a god, but you are **not** a god. You are just a man, and you will die at the hands of a man."

In history we cannot find the prince of Tyre. There is no record of a city with that name. It may have existed before history did or before there were written records of history. The prince of **Tyre** could have been *Nimrod*. He began to build cities and was so arrogant that he thought of himself more than just a human. Could it be *Nimrod*? He boasted he was a god and bragged about his great strength and power. He was no god. He was just a very conceited human being. God said. to him, "You are not a god. You are just a man, and you shall be brought down low to the grave and Hell will rise up to meet you."

Nimrod was just a man, but what was the true power behind him? God knew and began to speak to the king standing in the shadows behind the prince. I find it interesting that God first spoke to the prince of Tyre, and He established the fact that the prince was not a god but just a man who had deluded himself into thinking that he was an all-powerful and completely invincible being.

This prince believed no one could come against him and defeat him. He had everyone worshipping and following him. In return, man put his faith and trust in the prince of *Tyre* and loyally followed him. God informed this tyrant, this prince of **Tyre**, he would be brought down low and men would cast him down. God warned him, "You will die at the hands of a man." What a tremendous blow to his ego this must have been!

Afterwards God directed His attention to the power behind the prince. He then talked to the king of **Tyre**. This very important conversation can be found in **Ezekiel 28**. God told this king how he had been on the holy mountain of God and walked in the midst of the stones of fire. Every precious stone was once his covering. In reading, we discover that the king of Tyre was none other than Lucifer (or Satan as you know him today).

Lucifer was once the anointed cherub, the most powerful of all creation.

He was even greater than **Michael**, the *great archangel and prince of Israel*. He was greater than **Gabriel** the *messenger of God*. Scripture says *Lucifer* was created perfect and the sum of wisdom was a full measure. His beauty and strength was without equal.

Understand, **Michael** and **Gabriel** were *archangels* and were equal, but Lucifer was greater in position, beauty, strength and wisdom. He was given the position to be at the throne of God. He was the worship leader of heaven. However, this wasn't enough for him. He wanted to be greater than God.

He developed an attitude which got him cast out of heaven. He found a vessel willing to listen to the lie and be used. Through **Adam** and **Eve**, he regained the right to rule the earth. However, it was through *Nimrod* he made man a slave. It was through the willing vessels of *Nimrod* and **Semiramis** that Lucifer introduced a new religion to ensnare men's souls. Men were led away from the truth and relationship with God to stand naked before the Almighty without any hope.

Even though there is no history of the city of **Tyre**, it quite possibly could have been **Nineveh** with *Nimrod* as the prince and Lucifer, the king. After the destruction of the world by the flood, *Nimrod* carried on the tradition of **Adam** and opened the floodgates of evil with his rebellion and took to himself a title which no man has the right to do. He proclaimed himself God. He caused all men to go astray following after him instead of God. And behind it all was the clever manipulation of Lucifer.

Today the occult is spread far and wide. There are pagans and neo-pagans, wiccans, witches and Satanists. New Agers and others claim they have a way to God and dismiss the only way which is through Jesus Christ.

The hearts of the people are not believing in the creator who brings peace.

All other gods bring forth terror and wars and division among men.

Chapter 7

In spite of **Adam** bringing sin into the world and then *Nimrod* doing all he could by his own strength and wisdom to separate mankind from God, our loving God continued to love man. Because of a righteous man He spared mankind, and because of one perfect man He saved mankind. He knew man could not live perfectly, so He sent His only begotten Son to take our place on the cross so we could be restored back to fellowship and relationship to the Father.

Nimrod did all he could to separate mankind from God, but Jesus did all he could through the wisdom, knowledge and strength of His Father. He came to restore mankind back to God. Because of Jesus' faithfulness, loyalty and commitment to God, we now have an open way to the throne of God. We now have the wonderful opportunity to enter the Holy of Holies. We have the right to be in the awesome presence of our God.

Now we make our petition known to Him and are assured of a favorable answer. Truly we are fortunate and blessed to be living in this time. Nevertheless,

I see mankind reverting back to the time of *Nimrod*.

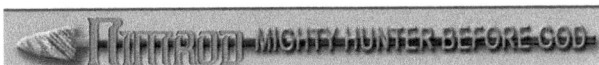

They are behaving as they did in the days of **Sodom** and **Gomorrah**. Evil is spreading throughout civilization as it did during *Noah's* time.

We find that man no longer follows the way of God or submits to Him. Man no longer walks in righteousness or holiness.

Neither does he pursue after a relationship with the God of creation.

Instead, man makes idols in his own image. He runs after icons, which have no strength in them. Each man goes after his own way. Scriptures says there is a way that appears right to a man but it only leads to damnation and destruction. Think about it! Today the occult is spread far and wide. There are pagans and neo-pagans, wiccans, witches and Satanists. New Agers and others claim they have a way to God and dismiss the only way which is through Jesus Christ.

Mantras, chants, prayer beads, meditations and yoga exercises will not get you to God. They also do not evolve you spiritually to become a god.

The lie to be a god is the oldest lie ever told to man. A creature, who was not even human, started it. The creature was once a beautiful cherub who was not satisfied with his position. The vain idea that he could become as God got him thrown out of heaven and eternally separated from his Creator. If Satan could not become a god, and he is greater in strength and power than we are, I guarantee becoming a god will not work for you. You are born a human and will die a human.

The **lie began** in *Lucifer's* thoughts, and in his arrogance he was expelled from heaven. The audacity of God to give Satan's position to a lowly creature such as man!

He went into the garden disguised as a serpent and retaliated against God by harming His greatest creation.

He told **Adam** and **Eve** that if they ate of the fruit they would become as God. How tragic that they believed the lie!

WE WILL NEVER EVOLVE INTO A GOD!

After the flood, *Satan* became more determined to annihilate God's creation and ruin God's plan. He found *Nimrod* open and filled him with pride and arrogance. He convinced both *Nimrod* and **Semiramis** they were more than mortals. He led them to believe they were immortals - a god and a goddess. They believed they were worthy of worship.

Once *Nimrod* and his family were dead, *Satan* continued the lie by convincing all the Egyptian pharaohs they were the **incarnation of Ra** - *the sun god.* He went to every kingdom of the earth and convinced the leaders they were gods, and because they were rulers, they were worthy of worship.

The **lie** has worked so well that whole religions were built upon it. These religions believe man is in the process of spiritual evolution, going from a vessel of clay, mere humanity to a vessel of divinity, to godhood.

In fact, one of the major religions today believes and teaches this doctrine as absolute truth. They refer to it as the **Adam-God theory.** This teaching states that at one time God was just as man is today. God, who was no more than Adam, through a process of spiritual evolution became *Elohim*, God of all gods.

Because of this evolvement, other men also evolved into gods and they all became the council of gods. This council got together and voted that Elohim was worthy to be God. As long as the council agreed, He would remain God. However, if they ever got to a point where they felt **Elohim** was no longer worthy they would vote Him out. His leadership and godship would be taken from him and given to another. What a lie! It is nothing but a doctrine of demons.

People want to believe this lie. The thought of being more than a man feeds their pride and provides self-gratification. *Nimrod* wanted to believe this lie. He had been given certain physical talent. He was strong, intelligent and had all the natural leadership abilities. But just being a leader was not satisfying his inflated ego. He craved so much more. Kingship was flattering - but not enough - and being just a man limited him. Instead, he yearned to be a god, and this desire caused his destruction.

His insatiable thirst to be god put him into the position as an enemy of God. Nimrod forced God's hand to pass judgment upon him. He believed the same lie as Lucifer did. He forgot he was merely a created being just like the father of lies did. Nimrod lost his kingdom and his life because of his pride and ego.

I don't care how strong or intelligent *Lucifer* was, he is still no match for God. Foolishly, he put his confidence in the lie and convinced one third of the angels of the heavenly host to come into agreement with it. Together they fell and are no longer welcome in heaven with any hope of ever returning.

Do not be presumptuous to believe that you cannot be deceived or that you cannot buy into the lie. Understand that the angels are greater than man and they were duped into believing *Lucifer's* lie. These angels who beheld God's glory and were in His presence when He spoke the worlds into being were beguiled by a smooth talker and paid the price for their covenant with him.

Imagine their surprise when they discovered they were not going to be god over their own universe. The *Mormon religion* connects with this train of thought. Founded by **Joseph Smith,** Mormonism believes in the **Adam-God theory**. Every male that is a *temple Mormon* believes one day he will be the god of his own world and his wives' duty would be to populate the world with spirit's children. Where do you suppose the root of the lie for Mormonism came?

It began with the heavenly creatures known as angels - not earthly creatures called man.

There are many cases throughout history where *Satan* has been able to con man into believing they were more than what they were created to be. We see many dictators who suffered from the sins of *Nimrod*. Every **Pharaoh** believed he was a god.

When God set the people of Israel free after four hundred and thirty years of enslavement under the **Pharaoh** of Egypt, He did it by sending plagues. Each plague was sent to defeat a false god of Egypt and prove to **Pharaoh** and his people that his gods were not gods at all. One by one each false god fell before the power of the God of creation. The final god to fall was **Pharaoh** himself. He believed he was the incarnation of **Ra - the sun god** - and had the power to reincarnate himself over and over again. Almighty God proved Pharaoh didn't have the power to raise himself or anyone from the dead..

When **Pharaoh's** firstborn son died, there was no power within him to prevent it or resurrect him. The revenge of the God of the Hebrews was just and demonstrated His awesome power.

Man should understand there is a spirit in the world that passionately despises mankind and is extremely envious of the relationship between God and man. Once this spirit being had a relationship with God as well, but because of his actions, he will never have it again. So, it is his goal to make sure man will not have relationship with God either.

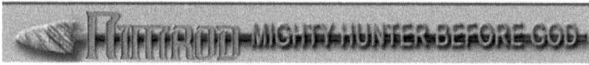

Satan is not stupid. He knows the power he once had and the glory he once felt will never be his again. He knows you were purposely created to replace him. He knows you are meant to be royalty. He wants you to make you a slave and keep you down.

Truly he knows you will never be a god and he knows you will not always be mortal. Someday, you will become immortal and be remade in the image of Jesus. Although you will never be a god, you will be far greater than the angels and what you are now. The body you have now is just a seed which will become a plant God has plans for.

In whatever form Jesus is in, you will be also. As He is, so shall we also be **1 John 3:2**. Yet, you will never be equal to Him. You need to grasp this truth. All mankind will spend an eternity with God and never reach His level of knowledge. It is impossible! We will be forever learning. We will rule and reign with Him. That should be more than enough for us.

We did not create ourselves or anyone else on this planet or in this universe. A loving God created all things. He put wonderful, wonderful things on this planet and put all under our subjection. He gave our father, Adam, the privilege of being the ruler of this world, but he forfeited this marvelous gift and turned it over to Lucifer.

God restored us spiritually through the sacrifice of His Son, Jesus. Then He gave to us the authority of His Son who destroyed the power of the prince of this world.

We have this authority so we can increase God's kingdom on the face of the earth.

In my opinion the secret to a successful life is rejoicing in what you have and not being envious over what you don't have. Give thanks for the blessings God has given you. Thank Him that you have been called and chosen to be a vessel of honor and glory to the Lord. Unlike *Nimrod*, do not strive to be what you were never meant to be.

Be joyous for you are being transformed into what God planned for you since before the foundations of the world was established.

You are now sons and daughters of God because of the blood of the Lamb. All other religions promise a future state of blessed; however, they present you with all sorts of heavy burdens and rules. It becomes impossible to live righteous enough to obtain what is promised you.

Praise God; His promises always come through. He paid the price Himself and now freely gives to all who truly believe. He simply asks for our obedience.

There is something severely amiss with man. It seems incomprehensible why man will continually rebel against a God who loves him. Man rebels against a God of love and endeavors to serve a god which only hates him and wants to see mankind destroyed forever.

Chapter 8

Why would man want to be a god? We cannot get along with one another. Each of us is too self-centered and egotistical. Instead of living in paradise, we would create a living hell. We cannot be God because we simply do not have - and will never have - the attributes, nature and the fruits that the God of creation has.

Neither could we handle the kind of power God has. The little bit of self-imposed power some leaders achieve ends up harming a vast majority of people.

Consider the people the pharaohs enslaved. For hundreds of years, the **Hebrews** lived in a nightmare of abuse.

Do you recall **Hitler** during **World War II**? He believed he was meant to rule the entire world and determined to bring into existence a master race. He brought destruction throughout the civilized world. Only by the grace of God was he stopped. Imagine if that demon-possessed, mad, mad man had been able to conquer the whole world. It would have been a hellish nightmare.

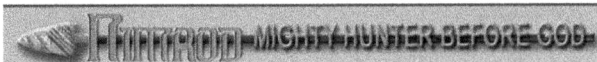

One Word Government

Despite the atrocities **Hitler** did, it is nothing compared to the leader of Chaos that is to come. We call him the *anti-christ*. He will be allowed to make war against the saints and to mock the God of Israel and of all creation. Just as his forefather *Nimrod* did, he will be allowed to proclaim himself God.

He will set up a **false religious system** in the world, and everyone who has the mark shall worship him as God. He will enter into the temple and offer up a blasphemous sacrifice at the altar - proclaiming he is God. He will break the treaty he had with the Jewish people and pervert the whole civilized world by commanding them to submit to him and receive his mark on their forehead or right hand.

This is the mark of the beast, the number of man, which is 666.

Nimrod was the forefather of this man who will come from Assyria - a country ironically <u>founded</u> by Nimrod

Just as *Nimrod* deceived and enslaved the world in his day, *so will his offspring*. The *anti-christ* will deceive many in his time. Those who will not humble themselves and accept Jesus, as their personal Lord and Savior will be easily led astray. Everyone will have no choice but to accept the mark of the *ant-christ* or be killed. If they do receive the mark they will be lost for eternity.

There will come a time in the very near future when the world as we know it will end and the reign of the *anti-christ* will begin. Nimrod ruled for a time period. God allowed him to go so far, and then he was conquered and destroyed. Pharaoh was allowed to go so far and no farther. He was conquered and destroyed. **Alexander the Great** conquered the entire world; however, he died at the age of *thirty-three*, and his kingdom was divided by his four generals into four kingdoms.

Rome conquered the whole world and established the peace of Rome which lasted for one thousand years, and then they were destroyed.

Hitler came to power and he conquered many countries. No one will ever know how close he came to destroying England, France and America. If God did not intervene on our behalf, he would have enslaved us all. God let him go so far - but no further. **Hitler's** kingdom came crashing down.

Time and time again Satan has tried to bring this world under subjection to him. He has a master plan to bring man into total bondage to him and to establish his own kingdom. Satan wants to receive worship. He still wants to be greater than God and exalt his throne above God's. God constantly thwarts him by allowing him to go so far and no further.

Finally Satan will set up his puppet ruler, who will be known as the *anti-christ* of the New Testament and the Assyrian of the Old Testament. For seven years (known as the **time of Jacob's trouble** or the Great Tribulation) he will torment the people of God.

He will conquer the world, set up his kingdom and force many to receive his mark. But God will say, "Far enough!"

Jesus will return to Earth, establish His Father's kingdom on the face of the earth and rule for a thousand years from Jerusalem. Those of us who do not buy into the lie of *Nimrod* and humble ourselves and call on the name of Jesus shall be saved and return with Him. We will rule and reign with Him for a thousand years as his faithful servants.

What a day to look forward to! His kingdom will be established forever. It will not be a kingdom like that of *Nimrod,* **Pharaoh, Alexander the Great, Caesar***, or the anti-christ.*

It will be the kingdom of Christ for all eternity. Sin will be done away with once and for all. The devil will finally be along with all those he used as a vessel. Those men who thought they were great and invincible gods will be tossed into the lake of fire along with death, hell and the grave. What a sight it will be when Satan bows along with the *antichrist* and *Nimrod* and proclaims Jesus as Lord of Lords and King of kings to the glory of God the Father.

We cannot even imagine the blessing and wonders that God has in store for us. We are limited right now to this little ball of clay we call Earth. Natural laws limit us. There will come a time when these limitations will come to an end. They will be lifted from us forever.

What will it be like for all eternity when we will be able to behold the face of Christ and have fellowship with Him? It will be worth the price of dying to self and living for God.

Nimrod changed the course of history on the earth, BUT Jesus Christ changed it for all eternity.

His restoring us back to fellowship with God will never end. Mankind has a hope and a promise of citizenship in the heavenly kingdom.

Jesus Christ, the Messiah! *There is no other name like His. He is the great Shepherd, Emmanuel, the Rock of Salvation, the Door, the Truth, and the Way. He is the King above all kings, the great deliverer, and redeemer. He is the one who came to give to us the victory.*

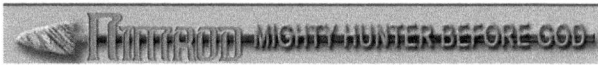

There are two roads man can travel in this world. One leads in the ways of this world. It is wide and easy to travel, but it is very deceptive - although there are many signs along the way promising wealth, prestige, fame and comfort. This road is paved with lies. At the end is only destruction, damnation and eternal separation from God, His glorious Son and His eternal kingdom. The other road is narrow and filled with difficulties, hardships and trials. This road is hard to find because few find it. Those who do find it consider it well worth the effort and cost. At the end is eternal blessing and fellowship with God.

We can only find this narrow road in Jesus Christ, for He alone is the Truth, the Way and the Life that leads to God the Father. Everyone will eventually make the choice of either damnation or salvation. Why not make the choice right now!

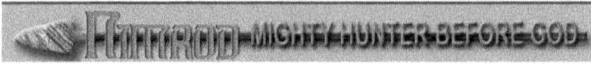

Accept Christ into your life today. Be restored back to God **in relationship** with him as His child and receive the blessing of eternal life right now. He is the creator of all things.

May the Lord bless thee and keep thee. The Lord makes His face to shine upon thee and be gracious to thee. The Lord lift up His countenance upon thee and give the peace. And they shall put my name on the children of Israel and I will bless them.

Shalom

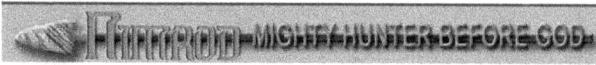

About the Author

Dr. Henry Lewis and his wife Patricia is the President and Co-President of an Apostolic International ministry called **Joshua International**. They have been married for 46 years and have two children and 6 grandchildren. Henry Lewis is a Sicilian Scottish Jew. His descendants come from Italy, Scotland and S Africa. Patricia is Canadian French, Native American and *German. Descendants are traced from Canada, Paris,* Switzerland, Russia, UK, Netherlands, Ireland and Germany.

Henry is a descendant of the famous Author and Pastor **Andrew Murray**. One of Andrew Murray's descendants named after him pastored in Fall River, MA

Dr. Lewis has authored 11 books which is still increasing. The first book called '*The Unholy Anointing*' which later was changed to ' *A Quest for Spiritual Power* '. It is now translated, in **Arabic** and **French.** Arabic version was printed and distributed in Egypt. French version printed in France and distributed in Switzerland.

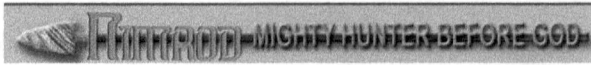

Dr. Lewis is a sought-after Apologetic teacher and author, teaching at churches and conferences along with numerous TV guest media outlets teaching on subjects such as:the times we live in, spiritual warfare, revival, revelation, the power of prayer. Henry teaches amongst international prayer leaders and former muslims. He holds three Doctorates in Counseling, Theology and Christian Education. His goal is to teach and train a courageous generation the incorruptible Word of God and introduce the power of the Holy Spirit.

Charisma magazine shared his testimony as a former political occult leader in 2000. 750,000 Hindus accepted Christ after this article was translated in their language.

To God be the glory. All gratitude is given to **ONE** faithful woman of 26 years who prayed continually until he broke free from spiritual darkness and abuse of seven generations of the occult government.

Henry and his wife have established churches in the US. Their first church under the Foursquare Gospel Organization was by the assistance of Aimee Semple McPherson's son, Rolf McPherson, who believed in their calling.

Later, Author, Teacher and Pastor Dr. Roy Hicks, Sr. (friend who worked at Angelius Temple with Aimee & Rolf McPhearson) supported them as well.

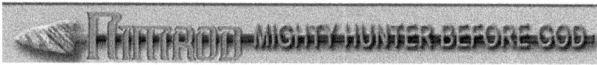

Their faith foundations also included from friends such as : Dr.Leonard Heroo (Apostle and President of Zion Bible Institute & School of the Prophets),
Evangelist Robert Schambach, Prophet David Wilkerson, Derek Prince, Lester Sumrall, Frank Hammond etc.

Their passion and faith put a deep thirst for the knowledge and truth of God's word in them which resulted in having a deeper relationship with his Lord and Savior, Jesus Christ – and not a religion – so he could hear and know the voice of God.

Henry & Patricia coordinated large revival transformation events in New England which began in Salem, Ma with the help of Rev Ken Steigler & local Salem clergy and Boston Brazilian pastors. Daystar programming promoted the events for 2 years with guest speakers: Bishop Robert Kayanja from Uganda and Evangelist Perry Stone. A transformation video was edited that shares the signs and wonders and miracles that occurred.

Dr. Henry Lewis is ordained with the Assemblies of God. Henry is also ordained Rabbi.

He is available for speaking.

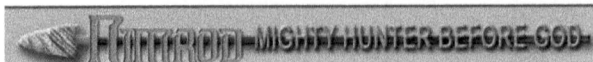

Available Books

A Quest for Spiritual Power- Redeemed from the Curse
(English testimonial)
A Quest for Spiritual Power- Redeemed from the Curse
(Arabic translated)
Choisi Par La Maitre - Called by the Master - (French translated)
Nimrod - How Religions Began by ONE man and how it applies
today
The Return of the Days of Noah - The time we are living in
The Dispensation of the Lion and the Lamb - The time for the
Lion is NOW
The Spiritual Opposition to each office of the Five Fold Ministry
Jezebel - What spirit was operating behind Jezebel
Run To The Battle
Praying from the Heavenlies and not from the Earth
The Names of the Spiritual Strongman and their Agendas

Available on Amazon under H.A.Lewis

Or click onto

www.halewis.org

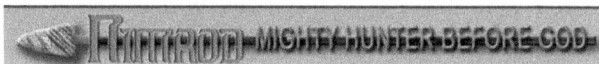

For I am not ashamed of the gospel of Christ: for it is the power of God unto salvation to everyone that believeth; to the Jew first, and also to the Greek.
Romans 1:16-22

The lie to be a god is the oldest lie ever told to man. A creature, who was not even human, started it.

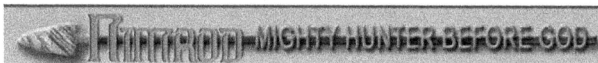

For More Information

In the US write:

Dr.H.A.Lewis
Joshua International
P.O. Box 742
Kodak, Tenn 37764

Email: Info@halewis.org

To order or inquire of additional products, visit us online

Website: www.halewis.org
Visit us on face book

Book Cover Artist: Debbie Wheat
Contact: **izayu54@yahoo.com**

Book Co-coordinators:
Grace Miller
Patricia Lewis

www.ingramcontent.com/pod-product-compliance
Lightning Source LLC
Chambersburg PA
CBHW060716030426
42337CB00017B/2884